C000141149

Other books in this series:
The Great Gift of Chinese Wisdom
…and Wisdom Comes Quietly
The Song of Life- Native American Wisdom
Timeless Values
Wisdom for our Times
Love for our Times
Taking Time just to be

Other gift books by Helen Exley:
Chinese Wisdom 365
Calm Days 365
Zen Gems

Edited by Helen Exley
Photography by Richard Exley
Designed by Martin Kerr

ISBN 978-1-84634-991-1
12 11 10 9 8 7 6 5 4 3 2

All the words by Pam Brown and Helen Exley
and the design, selection and arrangement are
© Helen Exley Creative Ltd 2015.
Published in 2015 by Helen Exley®
Gift books in Great Britain.

IMPORTANT COPYRIGHT NOTICE
The publishers are grateful for permission to reproduce
copyright material. Whilst every effort has been made
to trace copyright holders, we would be pleased to
hear from any not here acknowledged.

Our thanks and acknowledgements to the following:
Excerpt by THICH NHAT HANH reprinted from
Touching Peace by Thich Nhat Hanh, Copyright © 1992
Unified Buddhist Church. Used by permission of
Parallax Press, P.O. Box 7355, Berkeley, CA 94707.
www.parallax.org. Being Peace, Publ. Parallax Press 1987,
1996. Copyright © 1987, 1996 by the Unified Buddhist
Church. Peace is Every Breath, Publ. Rider 2011.
Copyright © 2011, by Unified Buddhist Church.
The Miracle of Mindfulness, Publ. Rider 1991. Copyright
©1975, 1976 by Thich Nhat Hanh. Peace is Every Step.
Publ. Rider 1995. Copyright © 1991 by Thich Nhat Hanh.
Full Catastrophe Living (Revised Edition)
by Jon Kabat-Zinn, Publ. Bantam Books, an imprint of
The Random House Publishing Group NY. Copyright
© 1990, 2013 by Jon Kabat-Zinn

The moral right of the author has been asserted.
A copy of the CIP data is available from the British
Library on request. All rights reserved. No part of this
publication may be reproduced or transmitted in any
form or by any means, electronic or mechanical,
including photocopy, recording or any information
storage and retrieval system without permission in
writing from the Publisher.

Printed in China.

Helen Exley Gifts, 16 Chalk Hill, Watford,
Hertfordshire, WD19 4BG, UK.
www.helenexley.com

Being
IN THE
Now

Reflections on Mindfulness

Helen Exley

If you want to conquer the anxiety of lif

...ve in the moment, live in the breath.

AMIT RAY

You should let go

and make yourself empty

and quiet,

clear and calm.

YING-AN

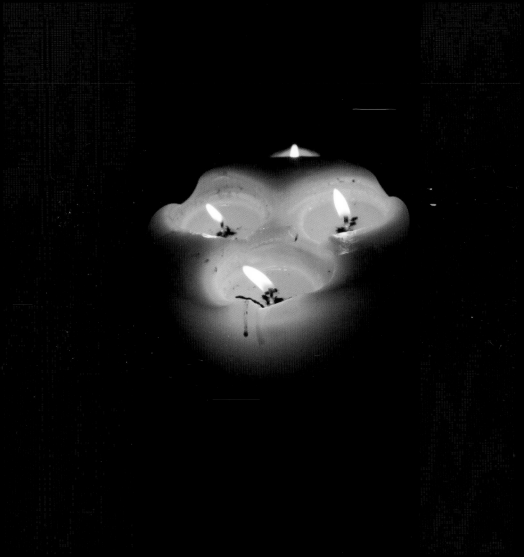

Between the in-breath and the out-breath
lies the possibility of the future.

RESHAD FEILD, B. 1934

Breathe out, look in, let go.

JOHN WELWOOD, B. 1943

Walk as if you are kissing the Earth with your feet.

THICH NHAT HANH, B. 1926

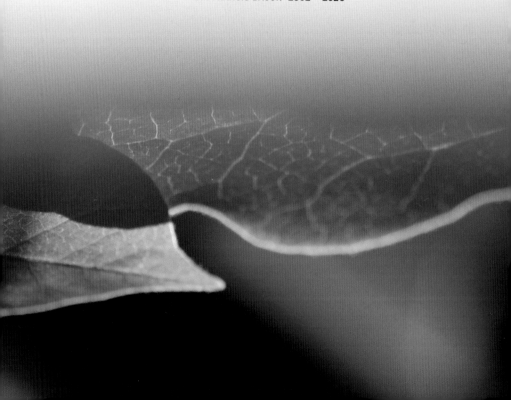

We have only this moment, sparkling like a star in our hand — and melting like a snowflake.

SIR FRANCIS BACON 1561 - 1626

It is eternity now. I am in the midst of it. It is about me
in the sunshine; I am in it, as the butterfly floats in the light-laden air.
Nothing has to come; it is now. Now is eternity.

RICHARD JEFFERIES 1848 – 1887

To breathe is a beatitude.

HENRI FRÉDÉRIC AMIEL 1821 – 1881

Give all you are to this moment.

HELEN EXLEY

Thus shall ye think of all this fleeting world:

A star at dawn, a bubble in a stream;

A flash of lightning in a summer cloud,

A flickering lamp, a phantom and a dream.

GAUTAMA BUDDHA c.563 – 483 B.C.

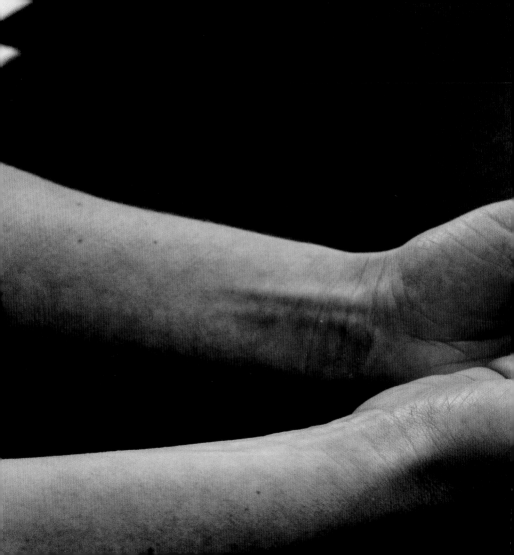

In meditation, we breathe in
the golden light of health and wholeness
and breathe out the darkness of pain
and suffering and hatred.

SUZANNE C. COLE

A spirituality of delight is one in which we will often say, "Ah!"

A Zen master once said: "Have you noticed how the pebbles of the road

are polished and pure after the rain? And the flowers? No words

can describe them. One can only murmur an 'Ah!' of admiration.

We should understand the 'Ah!' of things."

ANNE BANCROFT

a miracle

Our true home is in the present moment.

To live in the present moment is a miracle.

The miracle is not to walk on water.

The miracle is to walk on the green Earth

in the present moment, to appreciate the peace

and beauty that are available now.

THICH NHAT HANH, B. 1926

sacred

I wish that life should not be cheap, but sacred.

I wish the days to be as centuries, loaded, fragrant.

RALPH WALDO EMERSON 1803 – 1882

Among the mind's powers is one that comes of itself
to many children and artists. It need not be lost, to the end
of our days, by anyone who has ever had it.
This is the power of taking delight in a thing, or rather in anything,
not as a means to some other end, but just because it is what it is.
A child in the full health of his mind will put his hand
flat on the summer turf, feel it, and give a little shiver of private glee
at the elastic firmness of the globe.

CHARLES EDWARD MONTAGUE 1867 - 1928

All of a sudden you find

your mind and body

wiped out of existence.

This is what is known as

letting go your hold.

As you regain your breath

it is like drinking water

and knowing it is cold.

It is joy inexpressible.

HAKUIN

As you walk and eat and travel, be where you are.

Otherwise you will miss most of your life.

GAUTAMA BUDDHA c.563 – 483 B.C.

In Zen we are always told to leave the danger
of the high places and go on the path of safety.
That path means just ordinariness.

TREVOR LEGGETT

When you drink just drink,

when you walk just walk.

ZEN SAYING

Stay!

In meditation we discover our inherent restlessness.
Sometimes we get up and leave. Sometimes we sit there
but our bodies wiggle and squirm and our minds go far away.
This can be so uncomfortable that we feel it's impossible to stay.
Yet this feeling can teach us not just about ourselves but what it is
to be human... It goes against the grain to stay present.
These are the times when only gentleness and a sense of humor
can give us the strength to settle down...
So whenever we wander off, we gently encourage ourselves to "stay"
and settle down. Are we experiencing restlessness? Stay! Are fear
and loathing out of control? Stay! Aching knees and throbbing back?
Stay! What's for lunch? Stay! I can't stand this another minute! Stay!

PEMA CHODRON, B. 1936

Mindfulness is about love and loving life. When you cultivate this love, it gives you clarity and compassion for life, and your actions happen in accordance with that.

JON KABAT-ZINN, B. 1944

The beauty of the trees, the softness of the air,
the fragrance of the grass, speak to me...
The faintness of the stars,
the freshness of the morning,
the dewdrop on the flower, speak to me...
And my heart soars.

CHIEF DAN GEORGE (COAST SALISH) 1899 – 1981

The highest point a person can attain
is not Knowledge, or Virtue, or Goodness, or Victory,
but something even greater, more heroic,
and more despairing: Sacred Awe!

NIKOS KAZANTZAKIS 1883 - 1957

This isn't just "another day, another dollar."
It's more like "another day, another miracle."

VICTORIA MORAN

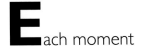**E**ach moment

a beginning...

Life is made up of

a constant occasion

of wonderful

new beginnings.

HELEN M. EXLEY

Without stirring abroad

one can know the whole world;

Without looking out of the window

one can see the way of heaven.

— The further one goes

the less one knows.

LAO TZU 604 - 531 B.C.

whole world

Silence

Listen in deep silence.

Be very still and open your mind...

Sink deep into the peace

that waits for you beyond the frantic,

riotous thoughts

and sights and sounds of

this insane world.

A COURSE IN MIRACLES

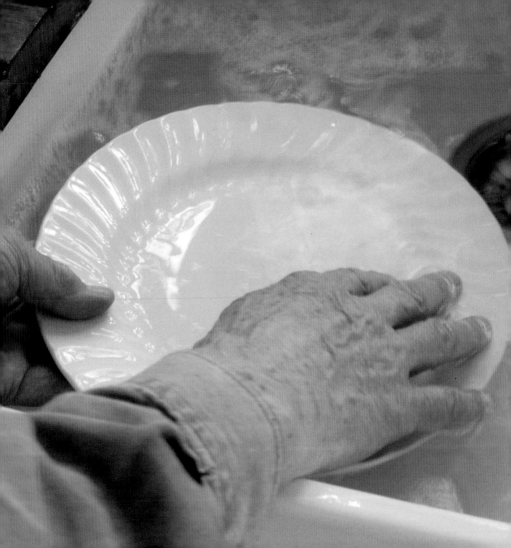

While washing the dishes one should only be washing
the dishes, which means one should be completely aware
of the fact that one is washing the dishes.
At first glance, that might seem a little silly.
Why put so much stress on a simple thing?
But that's precisely the point.
The fact that I am standing there and washing
these bowls is a wondrous reality. I am completely myself,
following my breath, conscious of my presence,
and conscious of my thoughts and actions.
There's no way I can be tossed around mindlessly
like a bottle slapped here and there on the waves.

THICH NHAT HANH, B. 1926

Oh, this is the joy of the rose: that it blows, and goes.

WILLA CATHER 1873 – 1947

There is great happiness in not wantir

JOY IS NOT ABOUT

LUXURY NOR FAME OR POWER,

ONLY ABOUT ORDINARY

DAILY EXISTENCE.

HELEN EXLEY

1ot being something, in not going somewhere.

JIDDU KRISHNAMURTI 1895 – 1986

Do we ever question the need to brush our teeth?
Or say, "Today I do not have time for brushing teeth?"
Can we go a week without brushing?
What would that be like? Please imagine it right now.
How will the mouth and teeth feel?
Do we believe if we brush teeth we will never need a dentist?
And how about putting in a comparable amount of time,
energy and regular practice to keep the mind clear,
fresh, and refreshed? Or regularly brushing and clearing
the mind from harmful residue?
I view Mindfulness as a way of maintaining mental hygiene
the same way brushing is needed for dental hygiene.

REZVAN AMELI

To see a World in a Grain of Sand,
And a Heaven in a Wild Flower,
Hold infinity in the palm of your hand
and Eternity in an hour.

WILLIAM BLAKE 1757 – 1827

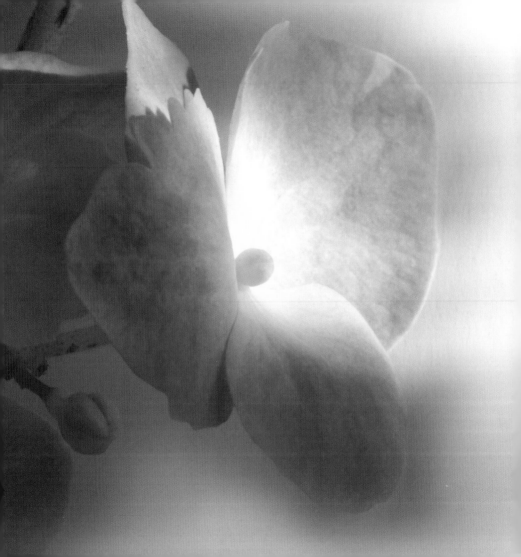

There are two days in the week
about which and upon which I never worry.
Two carefree days, kept sacredly free from fear and apprehension.
One of the days is Yesterday...
And the other day I do not worry about is Tomorrow.

ROBERT BURDETTE

We can easily manage, if we only take each day, the burden
appointed for it. But the load will be too heavy for us if we carry
yesterday's burden over again today, and then add the burden
of the morrow to the weight before we are required to bear it.

JOHN NEWTON 1725 - 1807

When I live in the now, I feel no real pain from the past.
Imagined fear of the future can't harm me.

JOAN BURKA

In Asian languages, the word for "mind"
and the word for "heart" are the same.
So if you're not hearing mindfulness in some deep way
as heartfulness, you're not really understanding it.
Compassion and kindness towards oneself
are intrinsically woven into it.
You could think of mindfulness as wise and affectionate attention.

JON KABAT-ZINN, B. 1944

Sitting silently,

Doing nothing,

Spring comes,

And the grass grows by itself.

OSHO 1931 - 1990

simply wait.

You do not need to leave your room...

Remain sitting at your table and listen.

Do not even listen, simply wait.

Do not even wait, be still and solitary.

The world will freely offer itself

to you to be unmasked. It has no choice.

It will roll in ecstasy at your feet.

FRANZ KAFKA 1883 – 1924

The mind is flickering
and restless, difficult to guard,
difficult to control.
The wise straightens the mind
as a fletcher straightens an arrow.

THE DHAMMAPADA

A wise person
does not value
a large jade
but cherishes
a moment of time.

CHINESE SAYING

The discovery is that there is no Great Knowledge

...ly seeing reality, only being at one with yourself.

HELEN EXLEY

You will never enjoy the world aright
till the sea itself floweth in your veins,
till you are clothed with the heavens
and crowned with the stars.

THOMAS TRAHERNE 1636 – 1674

The moment one gives close attention to anything, even a blade of grass, it becomes a mysterious, awesome, indescribably magnificent world in itself.

HENRY MILLER 1891 – 1980

Awesome

Speak nought, move not, but listen, the sky is full of gold,

No ripple on the river, no stir in field or fold,

All gleams but nought doth glisten, but the far off unseen sea.

Forget days past, heart broken, put all memory by!

No grief on the green hillside, no pity in the sky,

Joy that may not be spoken fills mead and flower and tree.

WILLIAM MORRIS 1834 - 1896

We are very good at preparing to live, but not very good at living. We know how to sacrifice ten years for a diploma, and we are willing to work very hard to get a job, a car, a house, and so on. But we have difficulty remembering that we are alive in the present moment, the only moment there is for us to be alive.

THICH NHAT HANH, B. 1926

Those who are awake live in a state of constant amazement.

GAUTAMA BUDDHA c.563 – 483 B.C.

I expand and live in the warm day
like corn and melons.

RALPH WALDO EMERSON 1803 – 1882

The aim of life is to live, and to live means to be aware,
joyously, drunkenly, serenely, divinely aware.

HENRY MILLER 1891 – 1980

Be present.
Be at peace as you work.
If you can do that then your work
will be done well.
Your thoughts, the values you hold,
will be in the work and will
permeate the whole process.
It will be good.

HELEN EXLEY

Don't evaluate your life in terms of achievements,
trivial or monumental, along the way...
Instead, wake up and appreciate everything
you encounter along the path.
Enjoy the flowers that are there for your pleasure.
Tune in to the sunrise, the little children,
the laughter, the rain, and the birds.
Drink it all in... there is no way
to happiness; happiness is the way.

DR. WAYNE W. DYER, B. 1940

You see, we believe that through the quieting of the mind

we are able to separate what is real and what isn't,

what is ego and what is truth. It is like making butter;

you keep churning and churning until the cream begins

to separate. You must really work at churning a chaotic mind,

learn to separate your thoughts from your true nature,

and become a witness rather than a party to your destructive

emotions. What you are left with is a natural state of joy.

natural stat

KUTENLA, BUDDHIST MONK

Don't seek,

don't search,

don't ask,

don't knock,

don't demand -

relax.

OSHO 1931 - 1990

"If it were just a matter
of playing football
with the firmament,
stirring up the ocean,
turning back rivers,
carrying away mountains,
I could manage it
easily enough"
said Monkey.
"But if it comes to sitting
still and meditating,
I am bound to come off badly.
It's quite against
my nature to sit still."

WU CHENG'EN 1500 - 1582

One cannot appreciate beauty on the run.
When I can be motionless long enough,
there is no limit I have ever reached
to the revelations in an opening bud.

VIDA D. SCUDDER 1861 - 1954

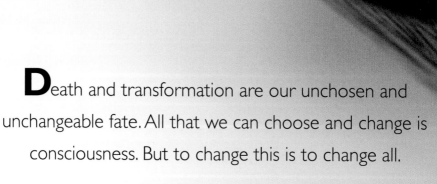

Death and transformation are our unchosen and
unchangeable fate. All that we can choose and change is
consciousness. But to change this is to change all.

RODNEY COLLIN

The whispers of rustling pine boughs.

Flowers blooming. The beautiful blue sky.

Fluffy white clouds. The smile of a neighbor.

Each of these is a small miracle of life that has

the capacity to nourish and heal us.

They're there for us right now.

The question is: are we there for them?

If we're constantly running around,

if our mind is caught up in endless planning

and worrying, it's as if all these wonders

don't even exist.

THICH NHAT HANH, B. 1926

The secret of seeing things
as they are is to take off our
coloured spectacles.
That being-as-it-is,
with nothing extraordinary
about it, nothing wonderful,
is the great wonder.

MASTER SESSAN

Normal day, let me be aware
of the treasure you are.
Let me not pass you by in quest
of some rare and perfect tomorrow.

MARY JEAN IRION

Earth teach me...

Earth teach me stillness as the grasses are stilled with light.

Earth teach me humility as blossoms are humble with beginning.

Earth teach me limitation as the ant which crawls on the ground.

Earth teach me freedom as the eagle which soars in the sky.

Earth teach me resignation as the leaves which die in the autumn.

Earth teach me regeneration as the seed which rises in the spring.

Earth teach me to forget myself as melted snow forgets its life.

UTE PRAYER

Praise and blame,

gain and loss,

pleasure and sorrow

come and go

like the wind.

To be happy,

rest like a great tree

in the midst

of them all.

GAUTAMA BUDDHA
c.563 – 483 B.C

...happiness should not be dependent
on things happening in the future,
on getting an amazing job,
on meeting Mr Right,
on owning a house in the country...
Happiness should be in the moment.

LESLEY GARNER

happiness

Happiness cannot be travelled to,
owned, earned, worn or consumed.
Happiness is the spiritual experience of living
every minute with love, grace, and gratitude.

DENIS WAITLEY, B. 1933

Life is but momentary

Life is but momentary,
whether you have the poverty of the poorest person
in rags or the wealth of the richest living person.

Life is but momentary,
whether you have the best of health or the worst.

Life is but momentary,
whether you have the most poetical temperament
or the most cruel.

SWAMI VIVEKANANDA 1862 – 1902

When compassion fills my heart,
free from all desire,
I sit quietly like the earth.
My silent cry echoes like thunder
throughout the universe.

JALAL AL-DIN RUMI 1207 – 1273

echoes

WHERE THERE IS PEACE AND MEDITATION,
THERE IS NEITHER ANXIETY NOR DOUBT.

ST. FRANCIS OF ASSISI 1181 – 1226

Lie gently in the dark

and listen to the rain pattering against the glass,

the swish of passing cars,

the hush of leaves.

Renounce decisions, speculation,

the tug of time.

The world beyond the window

enfolds your silence, holds you softly.

PAM BROWN 1928 - 2014

Life is fragile,

like the dew hanging delicately

on the grass,

crystal drops that will be carried away

on the first morning breeze.

DILGO KHYENTSE RINPOCHE 1910 - 1991

I am going to venture that the man who sat on the ground in his tipi meditating on life and its meaning, accepting the kinship of all creatures, and acknowledging unity with the universe of things was infusing into his being the true essence of civilization. And when native man left off this form of development, his humanization was retarded in growth.

LUTHER STANDING BEAR (OGLALA SIOUX CHIEF) 1868 – 1939

The fall of a leaf is a

hisper to the living. RUSSIAN PROVERB

To what shall I compare
this life of ours?
Even before I can say
it is like a lightning flash or
a dewdrop it is no more.

SENGAI

lightning flash

You ask why I make my home in the mountain forest,
and I smile, and am silent,
and even my soul remains quiet:
it lives in the other world which no one owns.
The peach trees blossom. The water flows.

LI PO 701 - 762

When I dance, I dance; when I sleep, I sleep;
yes, and when I walk alone in a beautiful orchard,
if my thoughts drift to far-off matters I lead them
back again to the walk, the orchard, to the sweetness
of this solitude, to myself.

MICHEL DE MONTAIGNE, 1533 - 1592

Let us not therefore go hurrying about and collecting honey, bee-like, buzzing here and there impatiently from a knowledge of what is to be aimed at. But let us open out like leaves of a flower, and be passive and receptive: budding patiently under the eye of Apollo and taking hints from every noble insect that favours us with a visit.

JOHN KEATS 1795 - 1821

Do we need to make a special effort to enjoy the beauty of the blue sky? Do we have to practice to be able to enjoy it? No, we just enjoy it. Each second, each minute of our lives can be like this. Wherever we are, any time, we have the capacity to enjoy the sunshine, the presence of each other, even the sensation of our breathing. We don't need to go to China to enjoy the blue sky. We don't have to travel into the future to enjoy our breathing. We can be in touch with these things right now.

THICH NHAT HANH, B. 1926

I am grateful for what I am and have. My thanksgiving is perpetual.

It is surprising how contented one can be with nothing definite –

only a sense of existence. My breath is sweet to me.

O, how I laugh when I think of my vague indefinite riches.

No run on my bank can drain it, for my wealth is not possession

but enjoyment.

HENRY DAVID THOREAU 1817 – 1862

only

nse of existence

Look to this day! Look to this day! For it is life,
the very life of life. In its brief course lie all the varieties
and realities of your existence: the bliss of growth,
the glory of action, the splendour of beauty.
For yesterday is already a dream and tomorrow is only a vision
but today, well-lived, makes every yesterday a dream
of happiness, and every tomorrow a vision of hope.
Look well, therefore, to this day!
Such is the salutation of the dawn.

SANSKRIT

Renew thyself completely each day;
do it again, and again, and forever again.

ON THE BATH TUB OF KING TCHING THANG 1748-1799

We sat together, the forest and I,

merging into silence.

Until only the forest remained.

LI PO 701 – 762

What is
the most
miraculous
of all miracles?
That I sit
quietly
by myself.

quietly

ZEN WISDOM

Sit
Rest
Work.

Alone with yourself,
Never weary.

On the edge of the forest
Live joyfully,
Without desire.

GAUTAMA BUDDHA c.563 – 483 B.C.

listen

Forget about enlightenment.
Sit down wherever you are
and listen to the wind
that is singing in your veins.

JOHN WELWOOD, B. 1943